Neptune & other poems

AF471813

Neptune

& other poems

Neil Young

The Whitefold Press

First published in 2012 by The Whitefold Press.

Copyright © Neil Young, 2012.
All rights reserved.

The right of Neil Young to be identified as the author of this work has been asserted by him in accordance with Section 77 of the Copyright, Designs and Patents Act 1988.

A CIP catalogue record for this book is available from the British Library.

ISBN: 978-1-291-05540-5

Typeset in Gentium Alt by The Whitefold Press, England.

Printed and bound by www.lulu.com

Contents

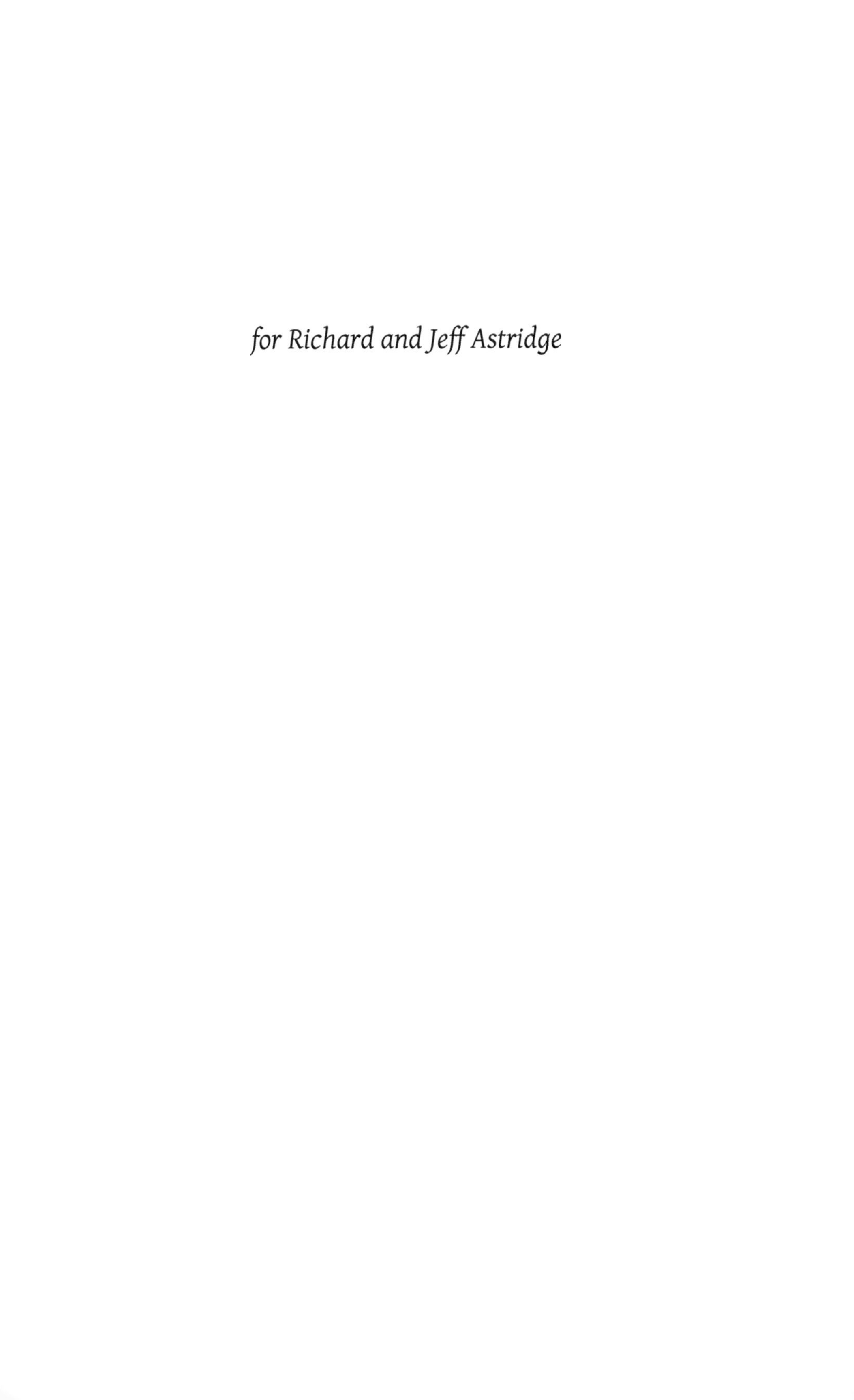

for Richard and Jeff Astridge

Neptune

(Based on the painting 'Neptune and his horses' by Walter Crane)

Curving now
And moving fast,
The wave rolls higher than the dead of war.

Growing now,
Gathering on
The tip of foam, a line of horses heads.

Faster now,
Their bodies, formed
Of frothing wave, exude quick scented madness.

Wilder now,
They touch the shore,
Webbed feet and white legs strong, race on in anger.

Smaller now,
Their manes dissolve;
Their bubble-eyes wash over shell and sand.

Inches deep
Their figures melt,
Retreat, with cursing eyes for war's deceit.

Further out,
Impulsive lines
Raise helpless heads, come charging to their death.

Skimming Stones on Hythe Beach

Evening simmered gently across the sea
Where the smooth white-blue sky melted seamless
Into it. A strange mist, light and patchy,
Blew across the stony beach; the process
Of evaporation drawn on the air.
At the edge of the returning tide, we
Stood selecting stones to skim, each with their
Own smooth oddities, flattened, polished, sea-
Worn, warm to our touch; ancient landscapes crushed,
Flung around the coast. We threw pieces back.
Some resisted the sea's rippling skin. Pushed
On, they skimmed three, four times, then sank. A black
Shaped cormorant watched, bleak-eyed, as mist blurred,
But those Martello towers stood undeterred.

Ancient & Modern

How well the old sits with the new,
Giving what is minimal
An interest and theme;
A neutral canvas
Where there is everything to learn.

How weak the new fits with the old,
Cheapening the substantial,
Marking out a struggle
Between bold principles
And inevitable entropy.

The Presence

(Based on the painting 'The Presence' by Alfred Edward Borthwick)

Gathered for communion, sanguine shadows
Huddle like culm before the altar. Those
Burnished 'big six', teasing out a prayer, shine
On the floor's bistered stone; each candled line
Smudging westward down the sombre nave. Light
Grasps the edge of a rising arch; its bright-
Ness fades in the vault's apparent absence.
The nave's flared nostrils imbibe transcendence.

Alone at the back, on her knees, she prays,
Head turned, her face a pale ceramic glaze.
His presence behind her brightly imparts
A blessing; her whispered concern departs.
Light once born in darkness, however small,
Dispels it; eyes once opened perceive all.

Beating on the Wings of Time

These eyes of age's grace
Return their presence to you
Like the gift of seasons.
Your feathered,
Fractured wings and face
Challenge me for reasons
Why swiftness' waste
Should spare my Saint Cecilia
And all the music that she makes.

Pevsner

(A Passion for Architecture)

Before breakfast, he'd polish his texts, then
With sandwiches, thermos and crumpled map
He, his wife would drive to each place of note.

He'd study buildings from the outside, note
Each feature that caught his eye. Only then
Would he venture in, mark it off the map.

Evening, at a borrowed table, he'd map
Out the structure of his words. Soon each note
Grew, bore his detailed, intricate style. Then...

...Then morning, the map, more buildings to note.

Ely

The cathedral, in silhouette, lays still.
Framed by a halo of low sun, its form
Ship-like, run aground, burns upon the land.

Nearer, it rises boldly from flat land.
Its stone, a two-tone grey and gold, glows still;
The sun defining shape where shadows form.

Within, the octagon's flame-roaring form
Pours down its intense streams of light; they land,
Searing ground, through dusty air old and still.

Ely, its still form dominates the land.

Tu es Petrus

(for St. Peter's Church, Seel Street, 1788)

Are you Peter,
        The rock on which eternal faith was built?
You *are* Peter.
        As a rock you stand, yet here stands nothing.
Your eyes are blind,
        Cold, devoid of bold coloured parables;
Your head vacant,
        A deconsecrated tabernacle;
Your ears worn deaf,
        Granite! The Lord hears no protestation;
Your voice, silent,
        Weighed in words, a disembodied organ;
Your body sere,
        Like stucco peeling, its fresco crumbling;
Your heart burned out,
        Dark, lonely, a hopeless sanctuary;
Your soul condemned,
        Cast down, suffers eternal mockery.
You are Peter,
        So how can this vacant shell mean nothing?

Beverley

(Three Snapshots)

i.

We took coffee outside the Lempicka.
A late afternoon sun warmed our faces.
Young couples posed in shades, designer shirts,
Far removed from all my expectations;
Cream teas, grey hair, tweed suits, crimplene and pearls.
We talked, sipped, watched crowds of people wander
Through the sun-drenched high street, working, shopping,
While the Minster, just out of view, watched us.

ii.

Beverley, York Minster in miniature,
Reduced to parish status, somehow lacked
Spiritual grace and power. Though everything
Fitted beautifully, the ancient gargoyles
Playing sackbuts, an assortment of flutes,
Embellishing the honey-coloured nave;
It made me feel empty, somewhat weightless.
I thought I'd float in an architect's dream.

iii.

From the north transept I sat and listened.
The organist performed a recital
Of works by Schroeder, Liszt, Roger-Ducasse.
Beverley's Snetzler-Hill organ possessed
Him, quickening his virtuosic spark.
Evening light interpreted each mood. Sun
Outside cast leaf shadows across the floor,
Softly spreading their mute gold-grey applause.

Shoe-horn

(In Memoriam: Dorothy Povah-Smith)

The language that he reads is esoteric;
Not hieroglyphs, yet symbols of high art;
Pages of black code that proffer colour,
Transcending each mathematical part.
Supple fingers play, they feel for spaces
To breathe within the dense, obscure inversions.
His hands form shapes, weaving as they translate
Chromatic patterns, pauses and progressions.

The language that I hear is also strange,
Warm vibrations, paradoxically chill,
Have power to engulf the stoic's senses,
Imparting peace with their hypnotic will.
Languids fizzle, rumble; chorus reeds roar!
The ancient art, an act of sacrifice
Carried helpless by Victorian echoes,
Re-echoing until the walls suffice.

The language that she speaks is stranger still;
Those weakened signals which in part connect.
Words from her stroke-afflicted mouth, slur;
In tongues she talks, a broken dialect.
Now a stranger's hands play, her substitute
Translating at the console both adore.
Stray manuscripts, half-thumbed, behind him root;
Beside them, those soft leather shoes she wore.

Recording Sessions

Take 1

Microphone levels
Set, the recorder started
Captures the next hour's
Fragments of organ music;
Jigsaws soon re-joined, faultless.

Take 57

Guy Weitz plays Widor;
Westminster 1920's.
Wax is warmed, ready
To record between clock strikes,
Footsteps, disapproving Priests.

The Easy Listener

Sometimes he forgets,
But today he sits at home
Conducting air, where
Sickly-sweet strings fill the room.
You'd swear he's Mantovani.

A Review Copy

Curious footnotes
In pencil mark odd pages;
Light, swift, difficult
To read. Some forty years old,
This book's histories unfold.

Fragments for a First Edition

(In respect of the book 'Poems Old & New' by Edith Sitwell)

The scent of someone else
Pervades the pages of this book,

That struck its beady eyes,
Waiting for prey to vulturise.

Bound blandly, slightly worn,
Unlike its observations born;

Words, like bone, linger on,
Whose language forms a skeleton.

Poetic fragments lay,
Their married scissor-shards betray

Thoughts on which we reflect;
A first edition's retrospect.

Reading Powell on Crosby Beach

(With respect to the poem 'Reading Proust on Aldeburgh Beach' by Neil Powell)

Shades are deeper here, less
Subtle than Aldeburgh;
This murky northern coast.

Anchored along the beach,
Gormley's zombies wait; dream
With the incoming tide.

Strange how they stand apart,
Their measured distances
Contrived. Their patina

Is rust; monoliths whose
Outlines are emphasised
Dark bronze by the sunset.

Like them, do we not stand
In search of another
Place; in search of lost Time?

Remembering

The distance between
Then and now can’t be measured;
Elasticity
Of Time, stretching. Memory
Shifts; retrievable, yet blurred.

The Burning

Out in the garden, burning rubbish, he
Observes our faces in the fire. Are we
Not needed in his life? Each photograph,
Each soul is licked by yellowed tongues; our grief,
A silent hell. Memory melts and flees;
A tree leans forth, stiffly conducts the flames.

Felling Elms, 1980

On Lower Breck they're felling elms:
'Diseased? We have been cured before;
Those surgeon's careful amputations.
Now she complains we interfere
With signals to her ariel;
Compulsive soaps a snow-like fuzz.
In thirty years, when digital,
They'll shunt their signals underground.
In thirty years, if replanted
Now, we'll be half the size we are.'

Triptych

i. Wake

His pale hand, so drained.
In his grasp, a yellow rose;
One bead of grief, dropped.

ii. Requiem

Sea-black mourners stand.
Floating on their wave of grief,
His coffin sails on.

iii. Reflections

This, a silent grave.
Reflections in the headstone,
Flowers for the dead.

Wallace:
On Viewing a Crime Scene through Photographs

(In Memoriam: Mr. Douglas Metcalfe)

How macabre! This photograph album's age
Unveils grim history in black and white.
My careful fingers slowly turn each page.

Hinged on grey vellum, each frozen image
Memorises that January night.
How macabre! This photograph album's age

Reveals their house as it stood, its visage
Time-scooped; 1931, sharpened, bright.
My careful fingers slowly turn each page,

And seeing her murdered there, centre-stage,
Bloodied, struck down near the hearth in half-light,
How macabre! This photograph album's age

Conceals her, laid in the morgue, her pale cage
Foetal-like, head shaved, a sobering sight.
My careful fingers slowly turn each page.

Her grey body protected the knowledge,
Who? Rigor faded, still she held truth tight.
How macabre, this photograph album's age.
My careful fingers slowly turn each page.

Monochrome

i.

The window, fixed between me and the world
Passing swiftly, projects its film sideways;
Old, monochrome, silent as early dawn.

Trees accuse dull clouds releasing rain. Dawn
Reveals in half-light our railways whose world
Of rust, factories, debris, slips sideways.

My eyes follow them in the gloom, sideways.
Below, rails glint, slither home now it's dawn.
Tired, I re-focus on another world;

A world entered sideways, often at dawn.

ii.

Now windows project their film in colour.
Fields in mid-ground, tilled, disguise crows. Their dark
Shapes flake from the earth; stealing seed, they fly.

A station, an abundance of trees fly
Past. Conversations overheard colour
This drab, beige interior. Sudden dark

Sucks the world away, whistles tunnel-dark;
Perhaps only a change of reel. We fly
Out the other end, same view, same colour.

In that colour, safe from the dark, we fly.

Traveller

You wrote this letter
Somewhere in the south of France.
I saw you, tousled
Hair untamed, sat on a wall
Warming yourself in the sun.

Your cursive hand stretched
Across each page; somehow it
Epitomised you
Stretching out over Europe
In search of goodness knows what!

You were a novice
Beatnik let loose on the world.
I thumbed through all those
Books by Kerouac, but could
Not see your need to escape.

What did you learn then
Busking with your flute on trains,
Taking refuge one
Night in a confessional,
Staring into her 'hot eyes'?

Sitting at your desk
In corporate gloom, do you
Remember this now?
Or that Orwell book I bought
You, the one you gave away?

A Young Seagull Observes...

I chance upon
A street lamp, where
In a daydream
He stares through me
From his window
Two stories up...

I look around
At his white desk.
He glares at his
Computer screen
That glares right back.
His eyes look tired...

His desk is full
Of worthless files.
He tries to think.
He looks again.
These barriers
Of language, glass

Prevent our talk;
Translation lost,
When I could show
Him how to soar
Above the dross
He deems is life...

Swans

Ten swans in a line
Mimic cyclists pedalling
Along the canal.

Closed Circuits

Strange metal birds perch
Hawk-eyed; their cameras turn,
Observe our small crimes.

Tortoise Eating Arugula

Tempted from his shell,
He reaches for the leaf, jaw
Clipping off a chunk,
Dark green, crisp and peppery.
His wrinkled mouth slowly chews.

The Maze

We carry your weight of grieving.
Whip cracks, horses kick into life;
Sad, distant faces in windows
Watch the boy lead this procession
Through unreal, sullen April crowds.
The dead roll away like slow clouds.
The maze of streets stretch onward, drawn
Like curtains; a cord of faith frays...

Terraces

Sullen houses
Trap stale air and smoking housewives
In their whistling, hissing kitchens.

Squallid living;
Rooms part furnished, jaded, frightful,
Proclaim defeat and apathy.

Weathered doorways
Mask the tempers, bottle anger;
Moods simmering, dissatisfied.

Surly tenants
Savour sex, bear violence,
Both visual and physical.

Darkened stairways
Break the fall of aggressive hours;
Rise, but fail to reach promised land.

Painful secrets
Whisper, leak from chimneys, skyward;
Unguent prayers for God's shying hand.

Four Meditations

i. Rosace

Some forgotten grace
Lights the window's leaded face
Filled with compassion;
Stains God's will upon the floor;
Blood of Christ for evermore.

ii. Organist

Dupre and Vierne
Hang and drift like incense mist.
Chromatic chords roar!
Tire his eyes, never his ears.
He tames the gallery's beast.

iii. Communion

We seek redemption
And kneel. The same old faces
In lines priestwards flood;
Mass-aholic Catholics,
Lips craving body and blood.

iv. Votive

Candles are glowing,
Hopeful, anonymous prayers;
Fears, woes, left in code;
Words the angels' eyes can read.
May God's grace fulfil our need.

Cobham Woods

Gnarled trunks rise up in lines like Gothic shafts of stone,
While underneath the weight of sky their branches groan.
Faint psalmody, those soughing leaves are clearer seen
Than understood; they quiver in a vault of green,
Reveal in speckled fragments, a soft, subtle light;
A clerestory up high, whose dusty windows might
Impinge upon the sullen shade to contemplate
The length of ground, uneven, nave-like, conformate...

The smell of leaf-mould, earth and sweet decay is stirred;
Its heady incense rising from the ground. We stand,
As if in some cathedral that nature's swift hand
Reclaimed; this holy place abandoned, barely heard.
Observe the altar just a burned out, rusted car;
Its shell, its subfusc heart, a brooding sepulchre.

Clouds over Sole Street

Our brooding, blue-grey visage slowly moves.
Below us, telegraphs, whose bronze wires thread
Their pensive silence, stitched from pole to pole,
Await the tickle conversation makes;
Language forgotten, whose signals, once thawed,
Will burn across our atmosphere grown pale.

The roads below lixiviated crawl,
Anticipate our movements, measured, calm.
We shadow them, their soothed, anointed skin.
Our meditations deepen as we roll;
As endless journeys on the land they claim,
So we possess the sky as dull as stone.

Vast orchards rooted in dark earth outspread
In reverential symmetry. They grow,
While we, the giants roaming god-like, play,
Observe them pious, petrified, despaired;
Their brittle fingers, stone like, bleached and grey;
Their knuckled prayers rise upward to implore.

Above the station we make our advances.
Worn platforms wear dark pools. Their old rains serve
As mirrors, mimic our approach, reflect
The moment our release is passed. Like voices,
Our notes of falling rain connect, dissolve.
Our songs flow out in rings, distort, refract.

Two figures pace the platform, disregard
Us, staring down convergent lines that run
On endlessly. Each sleeper measures miles
And minutes, their muted metal rails glide
Numb-mouthed. They shine with our increasing rain,
While poplars hush, anticipate our moves.

Still Falls the Rain

Weather turns spiteful, wild
Rain dancing in its brine;
Bloodlet Salvia stain
The rain-soaked bench. Rippled
Reflections of flowers
Pulse; mute drumming, show us
Swift rhythms in dying.

Indoors we overlook
This, in stagnant silence.
How long can the sky leak?
How slow Time passes since
St. Swithun's day's showers.
Still falls the rain. Noah's
Fears surge in us, sighing.

Iron

Spring lake; concentric ripples in the rain
Disturb a world reflected, while below
The skin's mirrored vanity hides deceit.

Summer lake; windless, smooth, pressed silky black,
Masks a surreptitious face thought serene,
Mimics soothed sky whose paltry wisps dissolve.

Autumn lake; garlands of fallen leaves sail,
Each offering to appease; each dead hand
Ignored, unheld and clutching no reward.

Winter lake; epidermis frosted glass,
A breathed on window in the cold; hard iron
Whose white sparks fly when hit, that thick-skinned Hades.

Memento

i.

Thunder!
        Purring like a thirty-two; †
Storm-clouds,
        Sagging, humourless and bleak;
Soldiers'
        Spirits on the verge must break.
Beaten,
        We crawl bellied over land.
Trenches,
        Sanctuary, stretching miles.
Flashes
        Strike for death beyond our heads,
Pumping
        Ricochets in bleeding earth.
Faces
        Of our friends, illuminated;
Others
        That we know, eliminated.
We wait,
        Each count lightening the load.
We wait,
        Mumbling our unfinished prayers,
Within
        The numbed silence of our minds.

† Thirty-two refers to a pedal organ pipe. Its pitch is so low that often it is felt rather than heard but can have a strong purring sound like distant thunder.

ii.

Footsteps in cathedral spaces
Melt among the organ's voices,
Where louring ranks insist we mourn,
And prayerful thoughts leave us forlorn.

Beneath my half-closed eyes, a tear;
This evensong's lament we hear.
Memories succumb to thunder,
Tearing our frail faith asunder.

iii.

Are we resolute when touched by God?
Hopeful, when there's nothing else?
Preyed on, being weak of mind and will?
How fate turns us towards faith.
Tearful in our disbelief,
Exasperated each nerve is struck.
Our fight is dissolved more
Than our unreasoning fear of flight.
What do we know? Beneath the sheen,
Do their tongues preach fallacy or faith?

iv.

Starlings startle the morning sky;
Breaking clouds despise,
Their end is nigh.
Wring forth your tears
Without vanity of reason.
Stand alone, assured,
Belief is not self-treason.
Float away, ill-humoured souls,
Exhale your wasted breath.
I remember...
                    ...their faces.
I remember...
                    ...the thunder!

www.ingramcontent.com/pod-product-compliance
Ingram Content Group UK Ltd.
Pitfield, Milton Keynes, MK11 3LW, UK
UKHW041834200726
13854UKWH00003BA/1131